FROM THE INSIDE OUT

LETTERS TO YOUNG MEN AND OTHER WRITINGS

Prose and Poetry from Prison

All proceeds from the sale of this book will be forwarded to

Restorative Justice Committee
Minnesota Correctional Facility-Stillwater
970 Pickett Street North
Bayport, MN 55003

Course Design and Instruction, Deborah Appleman
Cover art by Kenneth Starlin
Layout and Design by Lauren Sun

Student Press Initiative
Founder & Director, Erick Gordon
Teachers College, Columbia University
Box 182
525 West 120th Street
New York, NY 10027

www.publishspi.org

" By no means do we desire to gain personal glorification,
nor do we intend to benefit from a bad situation.
We stand accountable
and only hope that our efforts to redress our bad decisions
were not made in vain. "

Acknowledgements

This project would not have been possible without the vision and support of Erick Gordon, Director of the Student Press Initiative at Teachers College, Columbia University. Thanks to Erick's tireless efforts, the words of many student writers, both free and incarcerated, have found their much-deserved audience.

Thanks to Warden John King for his extraordinary understanding of education as correction.

We'd also like to thank the education staff at Minnesota Correctional Facility-Stillwater, especially Patricia Pawlak for her compassionate leadership.

Thanks to Carleton College for its generous support of a sabbatical year for Professor Deborah Appleman.

Thanks to Lauren Bierman, for her academic matchmaking.

Thanks to John Schmit, fellow traveler on this road and all others.

Thanks to Jimmy Santiago Baca, for inspiring poets everywhere, especially those who are incarcerated.

Finally, thanks to the families and friends of the writers whose work graces these pages. Your continued presence and support make everything possible.

From the Authors:

We'd like to thank tragedy, around whom our lives are based, and those who think about us, even if we'll never know it, and those who believe in us despite our hardened ways. There is one person who truly deserves all the credit for this project, but because of her sincere love for us she refused to let that happen... you know who you are... Thank You.

Contents

II. FROM THE WRITERS' PORTFOLIOS

III. ARTIST PORTFOLIOS

Foreword

These poems detail the hard-core upbringing of our kids—all our kids as we are all their parents in a social community. And they tell us we were not there to guide them, that we as adults didn't care so they didn't care. And how could they? Freedom mocks them at every corner in the neighborhoods where they lived, freedom of drug dealers to deal, freedom to get shot, freedom to die young. This is the grim tale as conveyed by young witnesses. When we try to tell them that freedom offers much more than oppression, they scoff and mention Abu Ghraib and Guantanamo. If they can commit crimes, I can commit crimes, is what they seem to learn so early from our most distinguished civil officials. And way too early do they learn that law enforcement means enforcing them, the powerless, to enter cells or graves.

So these expressions of poetry and prose come as a great relief for me because these young ones seem to defy the order of the day. They are not mentored, they will mentor themselves. They are not given opportunity, they will make their own. They are given no future, they craft their own out of deep felt words careful set into sentences that made poems that redefine their souls to the world beyond the walls of their confinement.

Just by letting us into their lives is a heroic step no social welfare or incarceration program seems capable to doing. So while all else fails, literature steps forward to hail the new day with their voices claiming they live, that they want a life, that they want redemption and a chance to make something of themselves.

Absent mothers and fathers, the bombed landscapes of their communities, the blood they spilled, all come forth to make an appearance in their house of mirrors, and with each one they make a reckoning, enough of one to make it a meaningful day, perhaps, a purposeful shot at a decent life for themselves.

Their lives like weeds break the concrete steps leading to drug houses. Their voices shatter the screams, the convulsing tears, the silence of graveyards, and cry for respect, demand attention, strip away the deception of official double-speak, and look the reader straight in the eyes and say, Listen to me, I have something to say.

I have listened and your words have made my life ever more connected to yours.

Jimmy Santiago Baca

NOTICE: Mailed from a MN Correctional Facility

Name: _Michael Jenison_

OID#: _191108_

Address: _970 Pickett St N_

City/State/Zip: _Bayport MN 55003 1-9-13_

Minnesota Correctional
Facility – Stillwater

UNITED STATES POSTAGE

$ 00.41⁰

02 1A
0004378506
MAILED FROM ZIP CODE 55003

NOV 13 2007

5505754001 C021

Cameron Coffee
Eagleton al Spings Wisconsin

ll..l.lll.l..lll..lll.ll.l..lll.l....lll.....lll....ll..ll

I.

LETTERS
TO
YOUNG
MEN

Letter to a Broken Toy:
A Younger, Forgotten Me
B.M. Batchelor

Dear Toy:

I have tried day after day to put this pen to paper, but my mind and hand seem to be working against my heart. There are little tiny pen lines on the paper that were the beginnings of unfinished letters that seem to form some secret hieroglyphic mantra that belies my intelligence. I have since fed that traitorous paper to the wastebasket that sits next to my desk and started anew. This time, I believe, my heart will work in conjunction with my hand and I can finally get these words down that have boiled on my tongue waiting to be soothed by your reading eyes. Please bear with me if at times I make no sense whatsoever; it sort of runs in our family.

I have forgotten you, stuffed you into that dank, dark corner of my mind where all of life's putrid muck seems to pile up, but your stench has seeped under the threshold and brought a miasma of memories that blanket my conscience. I want to befriend you, fulfill everything that has been left unfulfilled, and honor your memory, like the family of a fallen war hero. I'm sure you feel as if nobody could ever understand what you are going through, Toy, but trust with all of your heart that I know exactly what it is you feel. I know what your hopes are, I know what you dream of once your power is turned off, and I hear what you wish when you stare upon the Northern star. Believe me, I know; you are not alone. All you want is to be a real boy, not some puppet whose jerky motions are controlled by a mad puppeteer. How many times has your string been pulled and you spit out some internally recorded phrase that drips falsity, just to keep the puller satisfied?

On how many occasions have you been thrown into the toy bin, at times forgotten for days, left collecting dust while the darkness plays cruel tricks on your mind? There is no need to answer because, you see, I understand.

Let me say this, Toy: you are not a plaything. You're so much more than that. Your plastic can, and will, crack many times, but they will only add to your character. Becoming a real boy, or better yet, a real man, is a journey, but one that you can easily conquer with just the right attention to detail and some long-life batteries made of electric compassion and strong currents of persistence. You, Toy, can climb the heap of scattered and lifeless dolls, chipped figurines, and dented Tonka trucks to be you, and not you as in what the puppeteer desires, but you as in what your nightly wishes to the Northern star entail. You can be your own genie; you are the lamp, and all you need to do is give your heart a rub and let courage overflow your every being, let it seep into the plastic and let it turn it to warm flesh—the flesh of a boy.

You will only be broken for a moment, I promise. The wind will carry the dust away and the love of another will fill the cracks and leave you shining like the glow of a mother holding her new born child. You will have a new beginning, and it will be glorious, almost to the point where it will have you shedding real tears of joy, and you will feel the soft patter of your new heart spreading warmth and the breath of life. Oh, it will be wondrous, Toy.

So, please, believe me when I tell you all is not lost, you are not at an end; you are at the brink of a new beginning where there are no strings to be yanked any which way and no toy-bin to be swallowed by. The courage it took for me to write this letter I now bestow to you. Take it and drink it in; let it be your sustenance for life.

I wish you the best, plaything. I once kept you in a lightless place of my mind, but toys are never forgotten, really. Remember that.

With Love and Compassion,
A Real Man

Letter to Myself, Age 17
Warren Bronson

Dear Warren;

I'm writing this to you from 25 years in the future — a nice, round number. How fitting, seeing as how you hate math so much.

This is actually part of a college assignment, but my hope is that by the simple act of reading this, your future will not become my past. Believe me, my past isn't one to look forward to. There are a whole bunch of things I would like to tell you about that future, but you would call me a liar if they didn't come to pass, so I'll just say a few things that you already know but are still afraid to admit.

First off, that feeling you have of not really being connected, of not "fitting in" anywhere — I've not shaken it yet. You'll likely just have to ignore it, because you'll come to realize that "fitting in" is just a lame excuse for not being independent enough to make up your own mind. It won't really be too big of a problem for you, but it will get you into enough trouble to look out for it now. Eat and exercise regularly, because there's a good chance you'll end up diabetic. Your health and feelings are a lot more closely connected than even Dr. Gangsei knows now, so keep a regular schedule. Besides, your knees won't get any better without you staying in good shape, so get back into weightlifting, and start karate or judo.

Second, there's a reason the folks have never asked you what you want to be "when you grow up." They don't know, and deep down, they don't care. And they won't be of any help in deciding, because as far as they're concerned, you will never grow up. They are psychologically incapable of trusting each other, let alone any of their children. Dad was not allowed to grow up by his mother, so anything you do that is beyond his skills is just an excuse to be jealous and angry. There always seems to be an excuse for that. Ask either of your older brothers—they've been through this already.

As for mom and her "trust but go into histrionics," that won't get any better as long as you pose a threat to dad's idea of being "in charge." It just won't. On a related note, you will never meet the folks' approval. Whatever you do, there will always be a "well, you shoulda" from dad, or a "well, if that's what you want" from mom. It will drive you to distraction if you listen to them for very much longer. You already have a sense of what is "good enough," and yours goes way beyond what either of them can imagine: Set your sights higher than they are now, and don't get distracted by social bullshit. The ones who will remain loyal to you are the ones who are loyal to you now, and that won't change. You likely won't fit in on a path of social acceptance, anyway, but I've built a lot of respect for showing people how their "good enough" can be a lot better. And respect is a much greater goal than being accepted by some fickle peers.

I didn't find out I was good at anything until I was 30—your ultimate judge of how well you do is you. Not anyone except you. And you are a far better judge than anyone of what you think is the right thing to do, and the right way to go about it—trust me, you aren't far from finding out what you're good at, right now.

Oh—about that nice, round number. I remember very well how badly algebra and geometry kicked your ass a couple years ago. Find somebody, like Denis or Chad, to explain the Order of Operations to you and the lightbulb will come on.

Good luck, and I hope to see you in a different life than the one I have now.

Blessings,
You

Letter to a Young Me
C. Fausto Cabrera

I rewrite this letter every day in my head. So often, I have forgotten what it were like to be you. I have forgotten how you think and what you know. I understand you in such a different way. Like the main character of a movie I've seen a thousand times before. I know what's going to happen, but there is no way to get through to you. Yet I still holler at the screen.

I am not sure how this works exactly, or if it will even benefit you in any way but in hindsight. I have painstakingly considered the many directions I could take this opportunity and have come to realize if I squander these words it would be to spit in the face of God. So read it at least once a year.

I wish I could tell you that I am the hero you've envisioned in your future. I wish I could tell you all of your dreams came true. I wish I could say that I have no regrets and if you just follow your heart things will work themselves out. I wish I could tell you that things don't fall apart and not everything dies in the end.

Get used to pain; there is no way to avoid it so stop trying. Life seems so hard because we expect it to be easy. Confront adversity to the best of your ability for it will be the water to your growth. Try not to be indecisive; discern, decide and defend. If you are proved wrong, then chalk it up and say so. It is best to suffer in silence but it is also impossible, so find at least two ways to bare your heart. Trust no more than two people at any given time; those people might change, but if your wise, not more than three times. When you hit rock bottom, pick up the Bible and read it from cover to cover. Only when you have no where else to turn will you appreciate GOD's voice; shut up and listen.

Shut up and listen period. When you just wait to talk, most people pick up on that and will end up being defensive, taking the conversation nowhere. Seek to understand, and then be understood. Pay attention to whom you let around you.

Don't allow just anyone to get close to you, examine their qualities and make sure they complement yours. If they are not willing to sacrifice for you then they will never truly have your back Test them in small ways and just be aware of your options. It only takes one tragedy for everything to crumble; that may be out of your control but KNOW that there is nothing you can't handle! There is not just one-way in life, it is all gray unless you make it black or white. Things change so remain adaptable.

Okay...so this is getting kinda 'preachy' so here is some tangible shit. When you meet Katlyn, you'll know which one, get her pregnant and never let her go. She's got all the qualities necessary and has an indefinable capacity to love. Train to be the man she deserves. Separate women into two categories: Katlyn and everyone else. She's a keeper, trust me! If you ever meet a Sareda, run the other way!

In Super Bowl XLII, when the New England Patriots go undefeated to play the New York Giants, take all the money you have and put it on the Giants.

Dumb-ass! I told you! Here's another one just in case...Play the following Powerball numbers every day in March: 10-20-23-47-54 Powerball 26. If this didn't work, than GOD is on to us... oh well, I tried.

Read the following:

* "The Alchemist," Paulo Coelho
* "The Art of War," Sun Tzu
* "Iron John," Robert Bly
* T.D. Jakes sermons
* "Siddhartha," Herman Hesse
* "Things Fall Apart," Chinua Achebe
* "The Prince," Niccolo Machiavelli
* Carl Jung's theories

I appreciate your attention. I apologize to you for all of the shit I caused but hopefully this helps. If there is one thing I truly understand today is that the relationships you have with people are all that matters. There is no telling how long they will last so cherish the great ones and don't waste your time on the negative ones. If you follow this, that means the death of me. Thank you for sparing me of this hell on earth. Thank you for being better than me. I hope you find your potential. Try to be a straight-up type of individual knowing that 'keeping it 100' won't be understood by everyone. Now go tell everyone that matters how much we love them! There is nothing new in the world, it is just new to you and only for the first time.

Ohh…do me a couple of solids:
Punch your cousin Jay in the face as hard as you can,
And never back down from him.
Find out what makes Mom tick and write it down.
Last thing; be careful not to get stuck in the Streets bullshit,
They have no love for you.

A Letter to an Old Friend Whose Face I've Forgotten
Ezekiel Caligiuri

What's up Cousin?
I guess it's been a while,
those sweet watermelon memories
turned to empty years
and returned letters;
returned sentiments.

I was trying to sort through
grainy, overcast reflections
to remember
what it was like
when we were still friends
and our bond
was chain-linked to our destinies,
our ideas were too back then.
That was before
Our convictions became our convictions.

What's it like
in that big ol' city now?
Its probably not the same
as it was
when we were running around
as fast
as time-lapsed
images of a downtown night.

How's little Killer?
He's gotta be at least ten now,
damn, that's how long its been now?
Man those watermelon seeds sprout
when you're looking the other way.
I remember when he was born,
you smiled from ear to ear,

I would've given an ocean
for a small piece of that happiness
back then.

It would be nice though
if you would send some pictures.
I can't even see y'alls faces anymore,
not even in the dark,
hardened heart of my imagination.

I lost track of those memories
trying to see too far into the future.

Me, I'm still resting,
these people are still hiding my soul
underneath the courthouse,
under miles of dank sediment,
beneath some judge's backyard
and society's reciprocity,
in the middle of some town
in the middle of Minnesota.

My cousin asked about you
he just sent me a kite
from a Fed joint,
miles and miles into a forest
in the middle of nowhere,
in the middle of some town
I ain't never even heard of.
He wanted to know what happened
to those august days
drinking warm Colt .45
and gin from a bumpy bottle,
listening to a bad dub of
"Can it be
That it was all so simple then".
He asked if I had any pictures
but I told him
I didn't have any to give him,

and that I hadn't heard from you in years.
The last I knew,
you were in New York somewhere,
watching the sun rise over the Atlantic.
I gave him the address,
even though I knew
you hadn't lived there for years.
I told him I was still resting,
my soul hidden
in the middle of some small town,
in the middle of Minnesota.

How's your family?
I was sick
when I heard about your mom.
Things never stay the same
and burdens are exchanged.

I just lost my grandfather,
just a few years after my grandmother,
and I couldn't be there,
the only grandson
and I couldn't carry a casket.
Who's next?
How many more people is this bid going to consume
before a faceless society
gets its rightful compensation.

The fourth of July just passed.
It was sweltering
and I could hear the thunder,
the blasts for freedom
but I ain't free
and I wish for just a second
the world could hear
the clank of my chains.
Then maybe they could understand this,
then maybe I might understand it a little.

Man Cousin,
it really has been a while,
I really don't even feel
like the same person.
The tattoo on my arm
seems like a memento
from somebody else's life
and I'm not even sure
I'm still alive.
I yell my dreams into space
just waiting for a response
that never comes at all.
And man,
it's been six years,
pretty soon it will be ten,
ten turns to fifteen
what's gonna happen then?

I'm starting to sound like a convict.
I told myself I would never
swallow such a bitter pill
and here I am
in the middle of that same small town,
in the middle of Minnesota
counting my losses,
losing sleep over
what I'm going to lose next.
Most of it isn't mine anyways.

What's up with those pictures man?
I don't really think
I'm asking for a lot.
Just a few images
to kick start some new daydreams.

I understand
that I am not the "Hurricane"
and no, they won't make a movie
about my life

with Leonardo DiCaprio
starring in all the complex
moral situations,
with all the complex
moral dimensions
of my life
sorted through in 120 minutes.
Where in the end,
all is right with the world
and I can say it was all worth it,
my life was all worth this?
Leo would win the Oscar
and the movie-going public can go home
to their air-conditioned houses
and their smiling children,
knowing the universe
has balanced itself out once again,
and they are free
to dream their own dreams again
in a world where the truth
is still unacceptable.

For a little while
I was riding with a few cats in here.
I thought they were just like me,
walking the same empty corridors
and sharing the same lasting fears.
But I just wanted to break free
from all these
rules and restrictions,
and they just wanted to make more rules.

Your boy from Riverside is in here,
he gets out in a heartbeat,
but he'll probably be back
before anyone realizes he ever left.
I'll have something for him
when he hits the door.
He's becoming a real dirt-bag,

but most of my friends are dirt bags now.
I must be one too,
I wouldn't expect much else
out of this thing.

There I go
sounding like a convict again,
I guess I'm a convict now.
But anyways, can I get some pictures?
How's your life?
What's it like?

Letter to My Unborn Child
Elizer Eugene Darris

Dear Unborn Child:

I am waiting for you.
When you are born
there will be a place already prepared for you
at
The table of life.
This place will be inspirational, nurturing, cultivated, potent
and cultured.
You will know in the fibers of your soul
that you are safe.

When you are older and have children of you own sitting
at your knee
you will think back and you will tell them,
"My father always used to say _____."

I will fill you with the accounts of our Legacy of greatness.

Dear Unborn Child:

There is a place in this world
that is waiting on you.
This reality will be ripe for you to feast upon
because
it will be born from the womb of my struggles.
I will teach you how to love your self and others
because
I have experienced the bitterness that can seep
into you spirit
in the absence of this essential gift.
I will teach you to Create
the World you want around you
because

I have experienced the complete feeling of powerlessness
that can cloak
your awareness
in the absence of self-determination.
I will teach you to love
God and culture
because I have experienced the stark deficit
of
both.

To My Unborn Children:

Your Mother and I have names already
prepared for you.
Young Queen,
Your name will be Nia.
Nia has been chosen by your mother
when she heard it whispered into her ear by
your Spirit.
It is Swahili for Purpose.
Our names give us direction in life.
Every time you hear your name
you will be reminded of your divine purpose

Young King,
Your name will be Imani.
Imani has been chosen by me when it was whispered
into my ear by
your spirit.
It is Swahili for Faith.
Names give us direction in life.
Every time you hear your name
you will be reminded to have faith in your "self"
and
the Teaching that have been passed
to you
from me
by way of the Wisdom of your Ancestors.

Dear Unborn Child:

There is a place waiting on you that has been a long
time in the making.
It is an Intimate place
that is the result
of
pain and love.
There is a place waiting on you that has been born
from a promise of a brighter
tomorrow
A promise placed upon m life by
me
to
you
to build a World
for you to thrive in.
There is a place in this World
where your opportunities will
abound.
there is Life waiting on you.
Your Father and Mother are waiting on you.
We have planned for you.
Our lives are for you.
We live for you.
We cry for you.
Who we used to be
has
died for you.
Our
lives
are
for
you.

And you will ratify us

Tina/Chris
Joseph Davis

March 17, 2009

Tina / Chris,

Today is a melancholy day, and I wish I were able to speak with you two instead of having to write you a letter without knowing when you will receive it, or if you will ever even read it. If I were able to talk you two right now, I would ask how you are doing, and what are you doing in school. But most importantly, what are your plans for Tina's birthday next week.

I hope you two realize one day how important it is to keep in contact with your loved ones, for truthfully I did not fully understand this fact until I came to prison. My being in prison is the direct result of me not being able to control my emotions. I used to allow my emotions to run wild throughout my being, to rule my thoughts and my actions. Now that I have learned how to tame my emotions, I have found that I am better able to navigate through, the rigors of life.

Before I came to prison, my emotions used to rule my actions, now I actively rule my emotions. This does not mean I no longer feel. On the contrary, I am now able to better fully feel the entire range and depth of all my emotions. What it means is that I no longer allow what I feel to dictate my actions. I now meditate upon a subject and decide how I am going to act instead of reacting as a situation unfolds. Of course, life comes at you fast sometimes and sometimes you have to allow your reflexes to guide your actions, but most life changing decisions can be contemplated; and I would say, most all situations in life do not need an immediate response.

If there are any words I could share with you at this time, it would be to slow down and do not rush through life, enjoy every moment as it happens when it happens and try not to get too impatient with the way things are going.

This does not mean to become lackadaisical and put off striving to become someone better tomorrow then who you are today, but it does mean not to allow the stress or pressure of a rapidly shifting world to create the view of life you wish to focus upon. You must create your own identity or the world will create one for you.

Prison, drugs, and the addictions that kept me enslaved to a self-destructive lifestyle all stem from the fact that I was never in control of my emotions. So please Tina and Christ, guard your hearts and learn form me the need for you to develop your own emotional intelligence. Meditation and its reflective calming effects should also be studied and practiced.

Remember not to fill yourselves with great expectations for this leads to severe frustrations, which equals out to living a life of pain. If you do find yourselves hurting form the challenges of living, please try to find constructive ways to alleviate your sorrow. Doing drugs is a form of self-medication, and only temporary at best at its worst, doing drugs and/or alcohol leads to slavery and to living a life of hell. You will not find happiness at the bottom of a bottle—what you will find is loneliness and sorrow.

Tina and Chris, I love you two more then the world allows me to show. Sadly, I did not know what I do now, about emotional intelligence and drug addictions, before I came to prison, and this is not a good excuse, but it is a reason that even though I am currently in prison, I can honestly say that today I am free.

Life is beautiful if you choose to see its beauty and ugly, if you do not. Every situation is a lesson waiting to be learned, and sometimes the lessons must be repeated…Hopefully you will not have to repeat mine.

With love,
Your Father

"Docendo Discimus"
(We learn by teaching)

A Letter to My Little Pirate
David Doppler

Dear Zeke:

As a young sailor, it is easy to make mistakes and drift off course. While you grow older, there will be many mariners who trust so deeply in their knowledge of the sea, that they will feel compelled to force their ideas of how to sail upon you. They won't be able to resist offering up all kinds of odd advice and catchy phrases that they will insist are the answers to all of the sea's mysteries. Although she had good intentions, your great grandmother was one of those people. Like a vitamin, she would be sure to give me my daily dose of her immense wisdom before I'd set sail. Of her most notable was my favorite, "Red sun in the morning; sailor's warning. Red sun at night sailor's delight." Amazingly, the little rhyming verse seemed to accurately predict the weather. She also had others that I hated like, "Never say never!" She would always say it so matter of factly that I would be left seasick. Not to mention that the phrase itself is such a horrible contradiction. You will come to find that to be the case with most of people's opinions.

The truth is that life is about change, and there is no better teacher than experience. Right now, as your father, it is my honorable duty to motor around in the shallows by your side. To teach you port from starboard. To show you how to mind your draft, so as not to damage your hull, and where to properly place your ballast to keep level. It is my joyous task to advise you on the quality of your crew and how to keep the lens of your scope clean. Perception is key as you pilot your ship. For there will be many storms on the horizon. Stand fast! Search for a single ray of light, even when it seems the violent weather will never end. Rest assured, the roughest seas produce the most savvy sailors.

The sea is deep and its contents are beyond imagination. You will not be content with just floating on the surface. Take the time to dive in. Get wet and discover its wonders. Never be afraid to make "Never" your mantra. Never let the poisonous words "I can't" touch the same breath as your ability to achieve. Never be too quick to love or hate, and if you ever do, then never too much. Never owe a debt to any man, and when all seems lost, by any means, never give up.

Please understand that mastering the seas takes a lot of improvisation. The sea is an unpredictable story that you must author yourself. There is much I am unable to teach you. My only hope my son, is that before you set your sails to go out on your own, I have instilled in you the character it takes to always find your way home.

With tremendous pride and love,
Your Father

Redirection
(A Letter to a Young Man)
John Hesston

Only 14 years old,
And violence is your law
Poison by hedonism,
And a stigma of society,
Who squander blood money
You are a flippant fool
An embarrassment to the family
It is important for you to change
For your road is an eventual demise
You must be docile,
And open your mind
Recognize your flaws,
And seek to conquer
Learn how to use anger positively
For revenge is not justify
Resolve through talk,
And overcome your stupidity
By simple principle of rationalization
Evade from hate, discrimination, prejudice, judgment, and violence,
Because they are your enemy
Choose your comrades attentively,
And always put family first,
Because without them
Life is meaningless
Control your future
Your path is what you choose
You can prevail any obstacles,
Including yourself

A Letter to a Juvenile Doing Life

LaVon Johnson

Hello,

So, do you think you're ready to do this? Have you come to the understanding that you are now doing life behind bars? Life! The rest of your natural life will be spent caged like an animal. You will die in prison! And not one of the homies, or anyone from the click will be able to take your place. Truth is, none of them want to. Do I have your attention now?

I'm not here to preach to you or to try to intimidate you. I'm here to give you some understanding. And hopefully open your eyes to this reality we call doing time. What are you, 15, 16, 17 years old? Did you ever think that you would end up here? Did you ever think that the things that you were doing out there in those streets would bring you here? I bet not. You were so busy trying to put in work, or prove yourself for the set that you never thought about the consequences did you?

I bet you thought you were a killa too huh? But are you ready to deal with the consequences that come with being a real killa? You had the heart to take another man's life; but are you ready to sit down and face his family? Are you man enough to answer his mother's questions as to why you took her son's life? Are you man enough to look his child in the eye and explain why you killed his father? Can you withstand the emotional wave that your victim's family will hit you with; as they explain their grief, sorrow and pain of dealing with this loss?

Can you imagine that for the rest of your life someone will tell when to go to sleep, when you have to wake up? When you can go eat, when and how to spend your money: what to wear, how to wear it, when to piss, when to talk and how much you should enjoy it all? Oh, and I hope you like headphones because you will not watch another T.V. without them.

And what about the friends that the victim has that are locked up too? Are you ready to watch over your shoulder every day not knowing when they will seek their revenge? What will you do when your high school sweetheart leaves you for your best friend, saying things like, "Sorry, baby, but you're never getting out. What did you expect? Did you think that I would wait forever?"

You know what your friend is going to say don't you? "Man, you know I couldn't let that go to waste. Besides, it just happened. She was crying on my shoulder, talking about missing you. One thing led to another, and you know how it is? Now I know why you liked her so much!"

Is this too much to think about? With nothing but cell time for you to deal with you'll have plenty of time to think about it; or you could do something constructive with your time. You now have the rest of your life to grow and progress. Here's your chance to teach yourself what a real definition of a man is not what you thought it meant when you were out there on them streets. When you took that man's life you took on the responsibility and burdens of a man. You are no longer a boy or a child playing childish games. When the judge slammed that gavel, play time was over with!

This is a real, life, sentence. These are real bars and that number behind your name just became your new handle. Now you can become just another number, another ghetto statistic, or you can prove to yourself that you're more than just some number wasting taxpayers' money. Educate yourself with knowledge of self. Finish school. Get your GED or high school diploma. Maybe a college education as well, who knows?

You have your whole life ahead of you to change your view of yourself as well as how others perceive you. It's easy to give up and let the system lose you within itself. I've seen it done! I have friends who are so doped up on medications they can't spell or pronounce. They forget their mother's name as well as their own. I also have friends who I haven't seen since they went to the hole two years ago. They keep sending me messages to hook them up with new women, as if I went to the club last night or something. As if I haven't been right here for the past 13 years with them.

Oh yeah, you didn't know that part, huh? I was a juvenile when I caught my case too. The judge gave me life plus 25 years to do. So I know what I'm speaking about. I'm truly speaking from experience. I've done my share of time, of hole time, more than you'll ever do I hope. I'm not proud of it. It's nothing to be proud of. But I grew up. It's a shame that it took prison for the rest of my life to learn such life lessons. But it did. And now it is my job to share what I have learned with young men like yourself.

The most important thing I want you to get from this letter is: Don't give up. I know it might seem like everybody else has given up on you, that there's nothing you can do with yourself in here that it's prison. But that's not true. There's always hope. Hope that one day you'll be able to look in the mirror and be proud of the man standing there looking back. Forgive yourself for the things you've done to get you here. Forgive those who helped to influence you on that same road. Know that twelve people gave their opinion of the man they thought they knew. Only GOD knows the real you and he will judge the real you when he feels the time is right.

Until that time, you have work to do. Become the man your mother dreamed you could be. Change the opinion of those 12 people who prematurely judged you. Show them the man that you can become. Look for the change that you'll see in the mirror. Enjoy that change, embrace that change.

I'm proof to you that such a change can be made. There are others just like you and me. It's not an impossible task. Believe in yourself as I believe in you. That's the whole purpose of this letter. To let you know there is someone who hasn't forgotten about you. There is someone who does believe in you and your ability to change. But I can't make it for you. You have to want to do it for yourself. Just know that I'll be there for you every step of the way.

A Letter to My Little Girl
Lue Lee

You know, sometimes I think to myself that if I died today, would anyone notice? Would anyone noticed that I'm gone and would they even care. I look at it myself, as I am already dead to everyone already. Well, honestly, to tell you the truth, my life should have ended on that very same day that your mother's did. But somehow, I was given a second chance.

I don't deserve to breathe the same air that you are breathing right now. I don't deserve to live out my life and have me haunt your past, to bring up old memories of the past that you had already forgotten about and had left behind. Right now, I might be in the fault to bring all those horrible things back up into the light. But as I was saying, I don't deserve to be your father. That is why at times, I hesitate to even try to find ways to try to contact you at all.

On the day of your birth, your birthday, the celebration of the day that your mother had brought you into this world. It was suppose to of been the happiest day of your life. I can remember when you were born when I held you in my arms for the first time. Then on your first birthday, I can still remember the look on your face when your mother and I gave you your birthday present, it was a stuffed Pickacu doll, it lights up and talks when you squeeze his hands. Then the next day, the worst day of your life, you have to mourn the death of your mother. How hard it is for you, all of this is because of me.

I know by saying that I'm sorry is not good enough. There is nothing that I can do or say that will bring back your mother. What has been done is done; all we can do now is move on. Believe me, if there is a way for me to help bring back your mother I would, in a heartbeat. Even if it costs my life, I don't care. If today, I know for sure that if I were to give up my life for your mom to see you once again with her very own eyes, I would do that. Even for a useless breath in her grave right now, I would. She deserves better and more, so do you.

Many years had come and gone, many endless sleepless nights had passed. Still till this very day. I can't find the words in my heart to explain to what had went wrong, between your mother and me. Was it my fault, of was it hers? Was it because of the lack of communication or was it because we were too young of a married couple, that we both had made bad decisions with our marriage. And that is what had ended us as being together as a family.

I don't know if you would even want to even write to me or talk to me at all. But it's alright if you don't; I'll understand. What I might be doing right now is opening up some old wounds that were starting to mend up, I know this hurts. This chapter in both of our lives needs to be addressed and resolved, before either of us goes on with our lives. We both have to find out for ourselves, what the other feels and answer questions that we both have for one other for all of these years that we have wanted to know the answers to. Then we can close this part of our lives and move on.

I want you to keep this in mind; this is not just a paper for school or something like that. I'm not doing this for a grade or for recognition. I have been trying to tell myself to do something like this a long time ago, but just couldn't find the time. Well I, of course have all the time in the world, but I have been busy with other things. But it's no excuse though. When this opportunity came up, I jumped at the chance. I knew exactly who I'm writing this to. It's a part of me that I have been holding inside of myself that I wanted to get out a long time ago, but just can't find a way to. Also, the reason why I'm writing this because I hope that one day, someone either close to you will stumble upon it and will relay these words or letter to you.

You see, I can't have any contact with you, the friends and family on your mother's side. I can't have any contact with any of you. On that day, I lost all contact and custody of you. So I can't do much from in here, there is no one out there that will help me. All your aunts and uncles from my side all live in California. I don't have any family up here. So you see it's hard for me to do anything. This is why in the beginning I said that I am already dead to everyone around me. That no one would help me, help me to fight for you. The only fight I have left is to stay up here and in hopes that one day, you will want to know who your father is, and that I can hopefully tell you everything. Everything about what happened between your mother and me. Everything about what really happened on that day.

In the beginning of my sentence, I had contemplated about giving up. I thought about ending my life as well. But I then told myself that I couldn't. I could not leave you here alone, not knowing what happened on that day and why did it happened. Instead of hearing it from somewhere or someone else, you would rather hear it from me, the truth. To say, if I were to of die today, I would not go happy. I held this onto myself that I don't want to leave you with unanswered questions and have you look elsewhere for it, not knowing if it's the truth or not. I didn't want to be selfish, and I have made this promise for you, to stick this out and fight this battle for you. This is also the reason that I have decided to stay here and do my time here in Minnesota. I had a chance to do my time in California, but I chose not to. Because I want to be here close to you, so if one day you want to look for me, I am only a couple of minutes away. Also at times, I sometimes think about giving up, giving up this fight. Luckily, I have met and found some great friends that helped me to stay focus to stick this thing out. And those people are my real friends are the ones who's had stuck with me through all these years and helped me to stick through this.

Cyann, I know it's hard to hear all of this and I know it's hard that all of this is coming up again. It's like reliving a nightmare over again. I know that you were too young to remember anything. About your mother, about me and about the times that we had had together as a family. But I know that you can still remember your mother's voice when she calls out to you. A daughter always remembers her mother's voice anytime and anywhere. I can still remember the look on her face when she saw you for the first time. That was the happiest day of her life, also which that was the happiest day of my life was as well. You look almost exactly like your mother; you have her eyes and her smile. It is better that you don't have mine, what a bad sight that would be. But most of all, you have your mother's kind heart. That was what I loved most about your mother the way she overlooks my faults but see me for what I can be and become. She sees the potential in me; she never gave up on me because she loved me very much. But I'm sorry to say that I took her from you, from the both of us.

I had taken the only person that could have loved you more than me. I had taken a piece and a part of you that can never be replaced. I had done more damage than anything to you as a father. I have no excuse for any of this. Like I said, I hope that you will forgive me and accept my apology. I know it's hard to, but I hope that we can move on from this and put this all in the past. I still love you and I still miss you everyday of my life. There is not a day that goes by that I don't ever think about you, wondering if you are happy, wondering if you are safe, wondering if you are being treated right and loved. You are all that I have left in this world and all that's left of me. I would really want another chance to be in your life. We both had lost someone who we dearly loved. I don't know if I have also lost you on that day as well. I hope that we can get together some day and talk this out and become a family once again. Your mother will not be there, but she is here in both our hearts.

I know that you must have a lot of questions for me. I don't know for sure if I could answer all of them the way that you may want to hear them, but what I can promise and say is my answers will be honest and truthful from my heart, even if it may or may not have hurt me. I don't want to sit here and prepare a written statement try to figure out what you want to know and what questions that you might ask of me. No, I don't want to give you an answer as to which I had rehearsed it over and over again. I would pretty much rather answer you at the moment and at that time. I don't want you to think that I'm trying to somehow get over or get by this very easy. I don't, I don't plan on to.

Cyann, I will still be here for about another 20 something more years. I will continue to stick this out and stay out of trouble in hopes of getting out of here and to come home. I still have one more chance and I'm going to make the best of it. Like somebody dear to me once said, if you want something bad enough, you have to sometimes fight to get it. Also that God must have a reason for me because he didn't give up on me

Always remember my love for you is unconditional, no matter if you want me in your life or not, no matter if you forgive me or not. I love you, my little princess…

The Advice I Needed

Jason MacLennan

Dear Jason,

I need to start this letter to you by apologizing. I need to apologize to you for all of the negative choices that I've made that will negatively affect your future. All of the drug use and girls clouded my mind. Ever since mom died when I was 14 I went down hill. I just continually drank more and got high more. I got to the point that I felt lost in the world and didn't give a fuck about my life. I never even thought that I'd live to be 24.

The choices I've made will put you in a hopeless position that will make you callous to life.

I've made almost every bad decision a person can make. You're going to suffer immensely because of the pain I've caused the people you love, and who love you. I didn't think about how many people would be affected by my actions. I know you feel lost and alone. What you don't realize is that there are people in your life who do really care about you. You're going to throw it all away though because of a horrible mistake. Because of me you will spend your whole life wondering what could have been. You're going to break grandma and grandpa's hearts by taking away there family visits from you and dad.

Hopefully you'll be able to over come my mistakes to become a good man. You need to stay focused on your goals and stay strong. Don't get discouraged when things seem hopeless. Just don't ever give up. No matter how hard it gets, you'll always be strong enough to make it. You don't realize how much strength you have deep inside you.

I'm so sorry for the pain I've caused you and your family. I'm so sorry that you and your loved ones have to suffer because of my thoughtlessness. If I could have a chance to do things over, I'd do it in a heart beat. I hope that some day you'll be able to forgive me.

Sincerely,
Jason

To Baby Boy
LaVelle Mayfield

Dear Son,

You know how we do. May you live as long as you want and never want as long as you live. Where does the time go? I don't know, but it takes a lot of things with it. And before it's all gone, there are some things I've been trying to work out. I've been trying to put things in some type of reasonable order that are not completely understood.

There are those times when I find that I'm grasping at hints, looking for evidence to get clarity when no easy answers are forthcoming. I think the serious questions stem from some hidden insecurities rooted in our factors surrounding a lack of exposure and experience with economic success. In this life there are twist and turns, so don't quite.

As you grow older you will come to understand your blackness and what that means in America. I won't elaborate to much about that but, you will know the odds are against us gaining upward mobility; and you will also see some things concerning this that you will not like, witch may even tempt you to anger. Things such as injustice so unbalanced as to cause riots over verdicts and split a nation down the middle along racial lines; like a Rodney King verdict or an O.J. Simpson trial to have a nation cry out for his blood but at the same time applaud when a Mafia Don is acquitted on countless murder charges and heavy drug trafficking, but your cousins get 20 years for four vials of crack in my lifetime. Like I said, I won't elaborate too much on that.

These things can block cohesive thoughts to anger you but think clearly, many times the objective of others will be to simply get you upset. That is because they believe once you are, you won't be able to think straight anyway and will likely run away from your problems rather than face them, in fact, often enough they are counting on just that, something they were taught about you. They are prepared and you must be also.

These factors and others are designed to distract you from your destiny, keeping you unfocused, unstable, and heading toward disillusion, prison or death, out of their way in any matter. You must think on a higher plane of course. Keep in mind that even knowing these things frustration and impatience can wear on you. Be patient and don't be distracted for this can rob you of manhood.

Your manhood is not determined by any others standards, but we will discuss this later. For now think of Maslow's Hierarchy of Needs. Your basic niceties are what you need to stabilize your life and keep you sane. A foundation first is most important. What is a foundation in this instance? What is it used for? Why do you need it? A foundation is the basis upon which a person stands, is founded, or supported and in this case, all of them for a black man specifically, but anyone in general.

It is what you need to survive and base your decisions. And your decisions have outcomes witch will determine ultimately your fate, your children's fate, and your grand children's fate. Just imagine if your kids and grand kids are in prison talking about "nobody ever did a damned thing for me so fuck the world," what does that say about you as their father and me their grand father to think we didn't care for them poor or not?

That we didn't let them know that we have loved them for their entire lives, just like I have loved you for all of yours? I'm so proud of you, son. But understand, if what you stand on are false beliefs, misdirection, myths and ideals of no substance and things so far fetched and aloof you become an unrealistic fool, you will falter and fall. If you cannot stand, neither can your children or grand children.

So you need a foundation that is solid to help you achieve your manhood, and manhood is taking responsibility for your self direction and imparting your wisdom on your children, help them, but you can not stop all of their falls, just help them stand up again if you can.

I'm sure you have seen, met, or perhaps at times been that youth whom is selfish and unfocused, wilding out. For you that stops now. You will also find plenty of youths such as your self, even friends who have no interest what so ever in doing the right thing, no self direction without authority around to pressure them into doing right. Their foundation is self pity, chaos, and retaliation, taking no blame nor responsibility for their actions or consequences of those actions. And they hate any one whom has a since of direction and purpose; some one with a regular job.

If they are your friends, know there will come a time for you to separate your self, go for self and leave the pact behind. You will see youths of other races acting a fool and reckless also, but more than likely they can afford to do so. It is likely their futures are already mapped out for them or they have a relative in the system that will look out, maybe even some one to expunge their records if they have the right complexion.

You have none of these advantages and I can't give you any other than my wisdom at an early age in witch ever form I give it to you. It ain't all bad, you know how we do. Since you were a child I have given you these words by Rakim so that you would look around and be aware, ready, smarter, and strong.

To this end I give you once again, Friends.
Friends are hard to find so be careful
And I'm trying to enter your mind and prepare you
Though some ain't that bad
But some will back stab to get their fingertips on what might have
Despite the hand that feeds you, lead the people that need you
From those who hold you back or mislead you
To be a leader, don't get led on or led in
A wrong direction, a dead ends next then
You'll need a detour life's like a see saw
Ups and downs and I'll be there'll be more
Pot holes and obstacles in a path that's righteous
Sometimes you need your hands to fight with
This way of life
So straighten up and take your thoughts to places and never act two faced
Cause jealousy and envy you could find your end if you pretend to be
Temper, Temper, I'm off in the mental
The heart is strong but the body gets tender if the vibe I send ya makes you remember
Then paint a perfect picture so you can remember me
Though you could find your end when you pretend to be friends.

Love,
Dad

Dear Nephews
Terelle Shaw

Date: 3/17/09

Dear Nephews:

Despite spending more than a decade in prison I have been watching you both out of love and genuine concern. I have been hearing about your deeds and I am starting to see a pattern in your behavior. It is the same pattern of behavior that mirrored mine's when I was your age. If you do not defer from this pattern of behavior you may find that a visit to prison may very well be in your future. I am quite sure that you do not wish to experience this. There is no nightmare that you can dream that will be more horrible.

I worry about you even more now because you have reached the age when young black men enter into a world of social disenfranchisement and other forms of discrimination. Most of your fathers are not in the home so then it becomes a world of displaced and misplaced ideals of manhood which have their origins in pseudo-urban myths and is largely perpetuated by the culture of the mass media. It is a world where if you follow and not lead, peer-pressure will inevitably destroy what you innately can become. Your talents will be wasted engaging in meaningless gang activity, crime, drugs and women. This is the design of a political system diluted with historical, social, and economical intricacies that will lead you to the gates of prison. I have seen this modern day urban tragedy reoccur time and time again.

I entered prison when I was eighteen. The ultimate details of what landed me behind these walls have almost torn this family apart. For years I was frustrated and confused, but the time I spent studying gave me great insight and allowed me to understand the responsibility that I needed to take for my own actions, the role the family has played and the role that I nor the family can be held accountable for. We as a family are not totally innocent, because we have failed in the sense that we did not have an overwhelming desire to want something better for ourselves. This is the natural state of man. Hopefully, this letter helps break this vicious cycle. Ultimately, your futures wholly depend on it.

Even though you are children, you have a responsibly that is virtually impossible to achieve. You have to say no to gangs, crime, drugs and promiscuity. Yet these things dominate your current environment. You must resist them; you have to revolt against an entire cultural system that does not hold your interest at heart. What you will be saying is no to a system that defines these things as a rite of passage into manhood.

Furthermore, you will be left alone to make all the right decisions and if you make the wrong decision you will not be exempt from facing the consequences. This means that in order to survive this decadent culture every one of you will most likely become a product of your environment.

You have to compensate for your own inadequacies and the inadequacies of your mothers and fathers thanks the inadequacies of their mothers and fathers, of your communities and institutions, of your government. You will have to be the visionaries that will be left with the duties to secure your own futures because in the historically previous generations have failed you miserably.

I tell you this not to place a heavy burden up on you but this is the shape and color of our current reality. You are too young to understand that your government on every level debate on how much funding they should cut from the school budget, meanwhile your schools are already under funded and you're already undereducated and miseducated. Federal and state governments believe that building prisons and military spending is more fiscally responsible than educating the nations youth. They have cut social programs such as the arts, sports and community centers that hone your physical and cognitive abilities. As a direct consequence these viable institutions which sponsor positive mentorship in urban communities' nation wide have been replaced with negative influences from members of street organizations and drug dealing crews.

It is unfortunate that the wrong people are the most willing to take an interest in you. However, these are the people who you must avoid like the plague; these are the very people that will play a major role in the destruction of your futures. Oddly enough, they fill a void that is not being fulfilled in the community and family structure. While millions of young African American men are being led down the wrong path, pragmatic solutions are not being implemented to reverse this negative trend which have literally decimated two generations. This phenomenon is highly unfortunate when young people are in part, a viable asset to a nation's future.

Author Victor Frankl once wrote in his book, Man's Search for Meaning, that the abnormal becomes normal in abnormal situations. He said this in regards to the millions of Jews who were forced to steal clothes from dead people so they could survive the terror of the concentration camps during the Holocaust. This is currently what's going on in many cities across America; young people are forced to behave abnormally because their forbearers have abandoned them to an existence of atypical conditions.

I too have abandoned you, not consciously. Very much like you, the day I entered the urban reality I was ignorant of overall society. I responded to the conditions of my environment. I didn't rise above becoming a product when I was given the opportunity, instead I wasted my physical and mental talents to running with gangs and benefitting off of drug profits because I could not see beyond immediate sustainability over long-term sustainability, a mistake that I desperately regret today as I peer out into the world from my cell bars

However, you have a choice. The choices you have are that you can sacrifice yourself and suffer on the road to achieving the American dream honestly and respectfully which will take time and patience or you can advance your dreams hastily and destructively and without regard for your fellow man. But nonetheless, if you choose the latter there will be consequences for your actions and know that your family and community will suffer to which you are an essential part. In light of this, I will end this letter by asking this of you: always be on guard and do what is right.

I love you deeply

Sincerely yours,
Your uncle
Terelle Shaw

A Letter to My Son
Ross Shepherd

Dear Brandon,

My son. It has been twenty years now; so much time squandered, given away in a fit of rage. I am sorry for that. I am sorry for all of the time that we never had together as father and son. I am sorry for all of the things that you never experienced because of the mistakes that I had made and because of the price that I am paying for my heinous actions.

I am here in prison, now; regretting what we never had together. I missed your birth and the bond that your mother and I would have made with you in the first, early days of your life. I missed being able to see your little fingers wrapped around my thumb as I made a solemn promise to always put you before me in all things and to protect you from all of the bad things in life. I missed seeing your proud joy as you took your first steps, and the sparkle in your eyes as you tasted ice cream for the first time. I'm sorry. I gave all of that away.

My heart breaks at the thought of not witnessing you walking into school for the first time. I know that I would have been more nervous than you. I didn't get to hear you retell every minute of that day as I recall my own experiences from so long ago. I gave all of that away.

I missed taking you fishing with me for the first time and being so anxious to make sure that you would have a great time so that we could have something that we loved doing as father and son. I missed seeing the great, big smile on your face as you reeled in your very first sunfish on your Snoopy fishing pole. I missed out on seeing you jump in surprise at the cacophonous roar of a nearby lightning strike, and watching you sleep blissfully to the music of the rain. I missed your frightful tears after you were stung by a wasp. I gave that away.

I didn't get to see you dressed up as a Cub Scout or witness your recital of the Cub Scout Motto and the Law of the Pack in order to get your first of many patches. I never got to bring you to church to learn about God. We never sang hymns together. We never sang anything together. I never bought you a Holy Bible. I never got to dedicate His Word to you. I missed meeting all of the friends that you would make, and all of the activities that you would have participated in. I bet you would have been great at anything that you wanted to do. I gave it selfishly away.

I missed out on finding out about your first girlfriend through the grapevine because you knew that your uncles and I would have teased you until your face turned red. I missed being so proud of you at that moment, seeing for the first time the growing man you would one day become. I never got the chance to drive you and your sweetheart to a movie and then wait for hours in the parking lot for you to be done with your very first date. I didn't get to teach you how it is no big deal when she breaks up with you either. I gave that all away.

I never got to make sure that you did well in school, or to teach you about how important it is to be educated. I never stood over your shoulder as you struggled over algebra. I never got to feel happy for you when the lights went on and you finally began to understand it. I never told you how proud I was of you. Not even as you graduated from high school. I couldn't. I gave it all away.

I missed seeing you in the sharp Army uniform and the bitter argument that we would have had because I was disappointed that you didn't go to college. I didn't get to see you deployed to Afghanistan to fight the enemies of our way of life. I never waited up at night for a phone call that you had promised me so that I would know that you were okay. I never saw the change in you. I never saw in you what I see in myself when I look in the mirror. I never got to give you a hero's welcome home when your tour of duty was finished. I gave it all away.

Son, I am sorry for the things we missed. I am sorry for coming to prison and giving away all of the moments that a father and son should have together. Right now, I am suffering my punishment for the crime that I committed. I never knew until it was too late just how much was being given away. I am sorry that you never had the chance to be born. I am sorry that I never got to meet your mother. We never fell in love. I came to prison never having known love. We never had you; never got to see the person you would become. I gave it all away...

...Before we ever had chance.

A Letter to My Little Brother

Kenneth Starlin

I write to my little brother one single letter
That I may give to you the gift of caring
So many people, flowing like leaves in the sky
A limb, to a branch, working together in respect
Like a staunch oak tree in a forest of fear
Without each other the tree cannot survive

So long in darkness, losing the will to survive
The warmth of sunshine was found in a letter
I gave little back, twigs held back out of fear
Thin branches grew ambivalent, no power for caring
Skin, like iron hard bark demanding respect
Silent depths of the forest, hidden from the sky

Little spring resist the black stormy sky
Reach down to the depths with your roots to survive
The lightning and thunder will grant you respect
Sheltered, with love from this paper-thin letter
A single warm breeze fills your leaves full of caring
A single sunbeam to force back the fear

Never let your emotions be restrained by fear
Never allow your ambition to be bound by the sky
Send out each limb, Leaves sprout into caring
Roots entwining to help others survive
Rays of light from the seed of this letter
Feeding forest from the soil of unselfish respect

They tear off our branches without any respect
But never strike back with only your fear
When challenged return to the words of this letter
The darkness of loss will retreat from the sky
All fear will flow away and you will survive
Cultivating roots: protection by caring

Soul will grow strong with the practice of caring
Your world will blossom, treat it with respect
Without your compassion your tree will not survive
A forest stands firm against another trees fear
Together they drink sunshine from the sky
The paper that came form this one lonely letter

That you don't see me caring is the root of my fear
Your silence I respect under our shared stormy sky
With love our trees will survive with their roots in this letter

Letter to Isaac

Charles Yang

Dearest Isaac,

My son, where do I begin? I guess there's no where to begin but at the beginning, no one to blame but myself. For the longest time I accused everyone else for my circumstances and my short comings, not realizing my selfishness was to blame for the noose tightening around my neck.

I had a well upbringing. Grandma and grandpa fed me all I ever needed but I was never full. As a child, I didn't understand my parents' love. Grandma would beat me and grandpa would let her. Until this day, the emotional scars they've left me are still traumatizing. Grandma would scold me in the worst ways imaginable. I misunderstood it as them not loving me so I sought love and acceptance outside of my home. In my adolescence, more often than not, I sought it in all the wrong places. And in the pursuit of this superficial fulfillment, I embraced a misguided identity. So many years were wasted looking up to false idols, praising erroneous ideals and chasing fake friends to replace a love I didn't think I was getting from home. Before I knew it, I was down a road I could not turn back from, dizzy from those same fake friends and drug abuse.

As a child, I constantly messed up but was always able to fix it with an, "I'm sorry." My spitting out of the words so casually distorted it in my mind to where it no longer held any real meaning except as a means to get out of punishment. I figured when my parents hated me, they'd beat me accordingly but because they'd always loved me again the next day no matter how many times I screwed up, I could keep screwing up and they'd still love me. With this twisted, childish misconception of love, the people I considered most precious to me, I easily seemed to take for granted most of all. I carried this subconscious mentality with me into all my other relationships including my marriage to your mother. I allowed my selfishness to dominate my conscience.

In my arrogance, I dismissed everyone's advice and overlooked their warnings. I thought I could have it all but like so many before me, I was mistaken. I made allegiances that contradicted my responsibilities and I dragged everyone I loved and who loved me down with me including you. I abused my parents' love, your mother's trust and was absent for your childhood.

I remember the day God blessed us with you, November 12th, 2004. Before your actual birth, I tried to take your mother to her monthly check-ups, got her pre-natal care and tried mentally to prepare myself for you. Unlike your sister Callista, we expected your coming but also unlike your sister, when your mother was pregnant with you, I was already too far lost in myself. I can't even describe the elation I felt when the technician told your mother and I that you were a boy. You are 4 years old going on 5 now but I will always remember you as you were when I first saw you there at the hospital the night you came into this world, with your matted feral hair, scrunched-up face and tiny little hands trembling from your birth still. I remember cautiously holding you, fearful of breaking you and wrapping you up in your blanket. You were only two months when I left our family and regrettably, I didn't hold you very much after you left the hospital.

What I regret most of all in my life is how much I hurt you, most of all, your mother. And not realizing how good my life was. I was chasing a nightmare in place of the dream I already had. I would constantly tell myself that I would leave all the gang allegiances and drugs behind for your mother but I never did. And I would have my son, truly, I would have, I just didn't. Selfishly, I continued my stay in denial and believed it when I told myself, I had more time. But I was mistaken. I am not going to ask for your forgiveness. I just hope one day you come to understand your father, not for the tall tales and photos I left behind but for the actual man I am; I'm sorry to say more myth than legend.

I always loved you my son, you, your sister and your mother. You'll have to trust me when I say that I loved you even when it seemed you were the furthest thing from my mind and that I will always love you. The Hmong say that the role of the parent is to provide for their children a life better than what they had when they were growing up. I'm sorry to say I failed you. I hope this letter helps you to understand somewhat why I did some of the things I did. I was childish and foolish. Learn from my mistakes and do not follow my path. I thank you for your patience and your time.

Your father,
Charles Yang

II.

FROM THE WRITERS' PORTFOLIOS

The Mirror
B.M. Batchelor

I see beauty and vileness
Courage like that of a dwarf in a giants land
A rage that burns and tenderness
Depth like a deep ocean, countless as all grains of sand.

I see gallantry and a touch of meek
What stares back looks with determined curiosity
Braver than brave with the heart of Achilles' heel
Innocent haloed cherub with wings of monstrosity.

I see a war of heart and soul, truce of body and mind
He glares back unknowing, forgetful of my name
Accusatory and boastful, a caring serpent
Winter has a home in his heart, yet his eyes stay aflame.

I see hope floating stagnant anchored by scorn
Peace and serenity mingled with the acts of Eve
A hate that torments like calm waters; nevertheless,
Pride lingers there and reeks like a beautiful summer breeze.

I see the loneliness at the corners of his mouth
And a subtle nervousness hidden by a forged grin
Two pair of wondering eyes that define so, so lost
A stranger and dear friend, both who live to say—I finally found him.

Ten Minutes in the Desert
Warren Bronson

The battle had raged for millions of years, but this was the first time it caught the eye of the young man walking along the flat ribbon of blacktop that led home.

He looked up at the instant the sun dropped below the horizon, as it released its first desperate barrage of fury against the coming night—streaks of crimson and platinum and molten ice screamed skyward in ever-widening columns, hopelessly weakening as their distance from their source extended, becoming mere ghosts before being absorbed far to the east.

Far to the east, with the eternally-deep might of the universe behind it, the tiny sliver of darkness that had kept itself quietly hidden in the shadows of this world slowly, confidently crept westward, absorbing the raucous exuberance of the sun's first salvo, then extended itself, a huge black cat stretching from a comfortable nap, rising slowly, majestically upward.

The second, third, and fourth attacks were mounted from the west, each a richer, more vibrant hue than before—white becoming champagne becoming crimson becoming gold—yet each inevitably grew weaker, cooler, less pronounced, until the last of the fury that kept the sun alive for that day was utterly spent, dissipated by the encroaching night.

Not a sound was made; not even the fickle desert wind that dances and whistles to itself dared post against the majesty of this daily struggle for dominion of this world. A tiny cloud drifted silently northward, just above the horizon, reflecting the terrible strife that continued far beyond the young man's sight.

The young man shivered, suddenly chilled by the weight of the deepening velvet sky. Time to get home.

Rolling Dice
C. Fausto Cabrera

I am never without choice,
No one said the walk was without pain,
No one told me to roam without the heat,
Nobody asked me to move without the world,
It is what it is, with or without redemption,
Cause I lived without any respect for life.

I'm the only one who was sentenced to life
Out of context, the jury made that choice
Those involved turned to the state for redemption
All burdens fell on me to compensate for the pain
The point of fingers landed and I was exiled from the world
The sun shines no more, but I still feel the blazing heat.

Raised in a society telling me to 'get the heat'
'Us or them' mentality, death becomes me for life,
While they snitched and opened up 'our world',
Perpetuated a lie, while in hindsight took back their choice,
They think they'll dodge the repercussions of reaped pain,
They may believe they can hide behind the cross for redemption.

With me, there can be no redemption,
I live and die by my word regardless of the heat,
Regardless I'll take that, chalk it up and eat the pain,
Regardless I'll finish what I start and go hard for life,
Regardless of what they take, I have my choice,
And it'll never be to just comply with the world!

I cry over my former perspective of the world,
Matured, understanding the true cost of redemption,
I stand firm by the detrimental expense of my choice,
Cautiously moving forward respecting angers heat,
Experienced, learning to genuinely cherish life,
In the valleys and shadows of pure pain.

Getting to know myself was well worth the pain,
Sifting through culture, shaping my world,
Smelling the roses, living my life,
Hoping, but never expecting redemption,
Unforgiven, finding ways to cool the heat,
Is est qui est is, I'll live and die by choice.

Without pain, there is no redemption
In a world that cannot control the heat,
We live life only by choice.

Running Red Lights
(Inspired by the song "Stand by Me")
Ezekiel Caligiuri

I'm at a red light
on Bloomington and Lake Street.
My feet float on the interior of a passenger-side seat.
"Stand by Me" is dancing in the background
and the moon is the only light I see,
except hovering orange street lights
and burning embers
at the end of cigarettes
pressed between the fingertips
of passersby, lingering nomadically
on the street corners.

This moment paralyzes me
from feeling the emotions
I have come to this moment with.
Cuzzo is behind the wheel,
hiding behind something,
lost in his own preoccupations.
He's crazy,
We just don't know it yet.
His insanity will expose itself
later on in our stories.
Even I can't see past the glossed over
shields covering the feelings in his eyes.

I can see
the growing impulse in his feet
to accelerate across Lake street.
Whatever he does
I won't be afraid,
no I won't be afraid.
And I won't cry
I swear to God

I won't shed a tear.

Cars pass through the intersection.
I see myself as one of the fleeting figures
just passing by,
or just hanging out.
At any point we could
run this red light
and the break in the music will hit,
violins ushering a daydream
of being swung in circles
from the force of a Subaru
or side-swiped by a red Mitsubishi
and being trapped between pavement
and invisible flames.
Where there's nowhere to go.

Our options are wrapped in abstract
hues of dark blues and crimson.
To the west
is the million miles of stone road
meant to take us to the desert.
empty eggshell promises in abandoned department store landmarks,
an employment office that used to post in dull neon "25 cent Videos,"
and dark spaces to wring out
any of the light still fighting in your soul.

Car lots
with signs bearing names of someones
dead and gone, a façade
for a place where death is purchased.
And school-age children
rock butcher-knife creases in jeans
they probably will never wear to school.
They hang around,
waiting for one of those moments,
rife with adventure and consequence
to fall into their empty lives.
That used to be us,

That used to be me.
Except my burdens are a little sharper now,
my Nikes a little cleaner,
my soul a little dirtier now.

We could keep going,
hope the desert strips us naked
of the tainted clothes we wear.
Hope it gives us a new home, a new life.

To the east is the river.
We drive under highways erected for escapes,
past grocery Super stores
and naked lots
without the commercial value they once had.
Someone's fighting
with a homeless man
at a booth in the White Castle,
whose madness ruined his only cup of coffee.
It sits alone, untouched
strong and black.

Across the street
someone's mom is dancing on the bar
at the Poodle Club,
flashing her tits to
other confused, opportunistic patrons.
Tomorrow
She'll go back to her bible,
back to her grandchildren.

We'll just keep going
until we catch the river
and cross over into that other world,
with its own problems,
its own ghosts
where we are just visitors.
Maybe we can hide
with the dead already walking down Selby.

Still, there's no new home for us here,
just rented tenements,
where new tenants pass through every day
and we can't be someone
we haven't already been.

We don't know what's behind us anymore.
it could be death,
an evil force on our backs.
The breaking down of soft matter,
opening doors into dim-lit rooms
of electric and violent possibilities.
The weight of being alive
abounds in every moment,
in every action.
But that moment is dead,
that place is gone now.

In another heavy moment
like the heavy oil painting of experience
inside of single tear drops
we'll be through this red light,
north down Bloomington avenue
past deteriorating apartment complexes
Where people supplement menial wages
with pharmaceuticals cooked in their own kitchens,
on gas stove tops.
and families sit in stuffed spaces
because there's nowhere else to go
to escape the prisons of their poverty.
And like us,
they are praying that their yesterdays will crumble
into the sea.
And that the sky
that they look upon
won't tumble and fall on top of them.

We'll keep driving though,
past the Somalian grocery,

past the commodore,
beyond the cement conceptions
of ourselves.

We will turn on Franklin,
driving by women and men
pulling grocery carts
with full bags of aluminum cans
hanging from their mules.

The whole time
something might catch us.
The ugly face
of an ugly moment.
It creeps, as fast
as we let it.
Its pursuit inevitable,
its potential immeasurable.
But we can't look back.
The rear window is obstructed
with garbage bags
of worthless trinkets
that won't let us watch it
sneak up on us.
But we know it's there
anyway.

But we won't stop.
It's green lights from here on.
There'll be a whole lot of other
moments for us to forget about
on this night.
And the faster we go
the orange street lights bleed
into each other
into obfuscated lines,
and we blend into the night
but I won't be afraid.

A Chance to Fly
Elizer Eugene Darris

        set free.
When my eyes affixed upon this creature
it
resembled a bird's wings
that were
spread wide
and
it
appeared to glide.

I couldn't help but sit
and
be wholly transfixed
as I watched it
soar.
The creature noticed me spying and it let out a roar.
"This is a participatory accord!"
Its shriek pierced my senses
like the squeal of a boar.
Still, I straightened my back and stood my ground.
The creature eyed me curiously
before it huffed
puffed
and submissively
clamed down
When it spoke its voice echoed like a myriad of chords.
It said,
"All prospective scholars please get onboard."
        set free.
Without a double thought for safety or life
I jumped aboard and held on tight
(and, yes, I'll admit) with a tinge of delight.
As the creature and I
maintained our flight,
night melded into day

and day melded into night.

It warned,
"This is a free ride
but
you must direct the way.
Lest you will aimlessly ride
as your nights fade into you days."
        set free.
The creature confused me
every time
I heard it speak.
I thought,
"How could I control this beast
when I am so young
and I am so weak?"

It must have read my mind
because it spoke once more.
It said,
"Do you understand that this
is a participatory accord?"
I said,
"I heard what you said,
but pray tell what do you mean?
I am lost and confused
as we zig zag and careen!"

It said,
"A wise man once wrote 'Way leads on to way!'
That thought is much deeper
than the mere passage of days.
It means
pursuit breeds knowledge
and unleashes cascades
of the truth which is light
that forces
ignorance and darkness to abate."
As it spoke I looked back
at the trail that we blazed.

I was amazed
that I could decode
the symbols in our wake.
            set free.

It all began to make sense.
I began to comprehend.
I said,
"So the more light I seek
the more I will take in.
And the more I take in
the more I will understand.
And the more I understand
the more I can command.
And the more I can command
the more I can contain.
And the more I can contain
the freer my brain.
And the freer my brain
the more I can conceive.
And the more I can conceive
the freer I will be."

It said,
"Yes, yes this is true.
With me you can be free.
You see, I am every book, but I am also every key.
If you wield me properly
I can unlock any door.
I can tear down any wall.
I can resurrect any heart.
I can lift any spirit.
I can change any mind.
If you properly wield me
I
can
set
the
Whole
World
free.

Two Kinds of Heart

Joseph Davis

There are two kinds of hearts in every person; there is the selfish heart and
the selfless heart. Continuous improvement means to find the proper balance
between the two, so that a person can become self-constructive instead of self-
destructive…

Once upon a time, eons ago, a fisherman caught two different kinds of crabs.
These two different kinds of crabs were separated not by the color of their claws
or the size of their jaws, but by the kind of thoughts that they held within their
different kinds of heart. For it was their different ways of thinking that separated
them from each other and divided them into separate groups – if thoughts can
divide, then thoughts can unite.

The fisherman captured all of them because it was his job. He placed the
first group in a bucket upon the dock, and then put the second group in a different bucket. Both these buckets were actually prisons designed to keep the crabs
caged up together till it was time for them to be eaten. Since it was getting late,
the fisherman went on home to sleep and left the two different kinds of crabs
trapped in their prisons all alone overnight.

Isolated and separated from the sweet surf and sea, they began to feel the
hatred of living a life of full misery that would not allow them to swim in the
ocean and be free. The torture that they felt when they smelt the salt filled breeze
echoed within their songs of pain as they sang praying upon their knees. The
sound of the ocean's thunderous waves made them yearn to see their homeland
once again, before the morning came and sent them all to their graves. The moon
passed by overhead shining brightly from the sky; and them poor crabs could not
help but hang their heads low in sorrow and wonder why—come tomorrow—
they would all end up dead.

Now, what do you suppose happened at dawn's first light when the fisherman returned and learned, one bucket was still full of angry crabs, while the other bucket held no crabs in sight. How pray tell he screamed and shouted was one bucket still full, yet the other, all the crabs had escaped from out it!

Finally, the fisherman's question was answered by an old grey haired man who had seen it all happen before. The first bucket was still full because it was filled with a group of selfish hearted crabs, who hated one another, and who thought that each one of themselves was more important then all the others. They keep each other trapped in their prison—the bucket—with their self-destructive ways. For every time one of them would climb to the top of the bucket and try to escape, the rest would get jealous and pull the one back down again. In this way their selfishness kept them all in bondage and living the life of a slave. So the next day when the fisherman returned, they all went to their deaths in agony, for by noon they were all boiled alive.

The second bucket, the one that the fisherman found empty, was truly a prison without any prisoners. It held at one time a group of selfless hearted crabs who truly loved one another, and who really knew how to treat each other as a brother. The crabs in this now empty bucket believed in the principles of living a self-constructive life-style and utilized continuous improvement, for the betterment of all their lives. They figured out that if they lifted one of their number up to the top of the bucket and into freedom, then he could reach back down into the prison behind him, and pull the rest of them free. In this way they all made it away from the shackles of their slavery and thus they were all able to escape, back to the freedom of the sea.

There are two kinds of hearts in every person; there is the selfish heart and the selfless heart. Continuous improvement means to find the proper balance between the two, so that you can become self-constructive instead of self-destructive and thus live a life, free from the shackles of your own self-slavery.

Where My Memories Lie
David Doppler

The steps hide the light.
Questions angrily pace up and down
searching for faults in the madness.

The steps some times laugh at my stride.
Their convincing granite face towers my smile
and bites at my ribs.
This is only one!
Not 1 like me,
but one of the many I've tucked away
under the spaces between my words.

The steps, they know me now,
like fingerprints and snowflakes
I balance my soul to their skin.
Oh, they know me;
they have licked and tasted
the desperate flavors of my dreams down to the stem.
Only paper left now;
crumpled and balled up.

These steps, muddied and littered with memoir pieces
stuck and dragging from the end of my shoes,
waving through the cracks.
I'm standing there wishing they would just go away;
their screams and guts smear my purpose.

These steps, stained with my courage.
I've stopped to look back.
It's dried and trampled,
full of footprints from my pursuers,
in some spots thick and squishy
others full of worms.

These abandoned steps, sometimes silently cold.
My sighs materialize spirits stretched too thin
to show me the way.
They evaporate into my shivers,
so alone, I rummage through tear-soaked steps,
sinking in the "Whys?"

Say Goodbye

John Hesston

An alley that gets darker with time,
where a man sits to play
his guitar. Pleasant melodic tones
from strings resonating a song
that echoes from wall to wall.
Producing the sounds he loves,

triggering memories of his love,
a woman who's been gone a long time.
He has been encaged within walls,
and his only escape is to play
the guitar of a depressing song.
Each strum emits a different tone,

Somewhat infused with Spanish tones.
The style of music she loves
to dance to. Instrumental but a song
that brings him to a special time
where he could freely play
music without any barricading walls.

He lacks the courage to climb the wall.
Afraid to lose the only tones
of music he can play
to remember his only love.
He hopes to have the strength this time
to let go of the song

The encumbrance of the song
will never get him over the wall.
Hoping this is the last time
for him to recreate the tones
and seal all the love.
Once again, he starts to play

with tears streaming down as he plays
the same sad but melodious song,
and says goodbye to the one he loved.
Now he can see beyond the crumbled walls,
ready to compose new tones
for a new beginning and time

Music is his love and he will continue to play
for the lost time. Forget the old song,
the fragmented wall, and the sad tones.

A Promise of Justice: A Sestina

LaVon Johnson

My Grandmother's bible held all hope,
For here, through the Lord's word she found promise.
Not going to service each week is like failure,
bible study and prayer, is her life.
Choir practice and spiritual hymns her justice,
the bars on the church's windows her death.

A grandson serving life, her death!
No parole board equals no hope.
Who cares if he was 17, it's justice,
all she remembers is his promise.
Which is hard to keep while doing life,
causing me to look at myself as a failure.

Someone might ask, "What is failure?"
Not fulfilling my promise before her death.
Or not doing this whole life sentence and taking my own life.
She tells me in the bible I'll find hope,
I reply, "I'll make nan other promise."
She said, "Seek the Lord's justice."

What about the victim's justice?
I'm alive, so the trial was a failure.
But to them, what could I promise?
Their only request was my death.
And in that they saw hope,
but in that I saw life!

For after death there's eternal life.
As a spirit I'll find my own justice.
Maybe to others I can give hope,
in death I know I can't be a failure.
But what else can you call death,
except fulfillment of a promise?

What left can I promise,
maybe to try and change my life?
To stop worrying about my death,
to prove wrong this system of justice.
Showing that my life was not a failure:
That regardless of it all, there's always hope.

Death is not promised.
Even though I'm doing life there's still hope.
That the only failure is a senseless death!

Cyann: A Sestina
Lue Lee

I can't tell you how much I love you,
You are constantly on my mind,
You look just like your mother,
I wish that I can do more to be a real father,
Cyann, You I will always remember,
Don't worry little girl, this is not the end.

Don't look at it like it's the final end,
Each and everyday I would always think about you,
You are the last thing your mother remembers,
Be strong; don't let people play tricks with your mind,
Where ever you go, always remember that I'm your father,
Always remember that you came from your beloved mother.

Later on in life, you will become a great mother,
Don't worry, I'm still here, it's not the end,
Always remember that you do have a real father,
No one can really tell you what to do, only you,
Your beautiful smile, will always be on my mind,
It's hard to go back, but just try to remember.

Your mom is gone; she will always be remembered,
Always keep in mind, the name of your mother,
Mommy and Daddy are not there, it's not the end,
I hope that you will always have us in mind,
I'm here to answer what questions you have in you,
I always and will always be your father.

Nobody can love you like your mother and father,
I know that what happened, is hard to remember,
I lived my life already and I'm here for you,
Don't forget to go and visit your mother,
Forever always remember to keep us in mind,
This is not our family's final chapter; this is not the end.

You always be on your mother's mind,
When you grow up, don't forget to visit your father,
Your mother and I, our love for you will never end,
You will always be the one we both love and remember,
Life is hard without mom, one day you will be a mother,
Both our lives didn't end; we are kept alive because of you.

Your life is not at an end, keep that in mind,
For you, you now have taken the place of your mother,
Your Father, I will be the last memory of our family to remember

My First Encagement

Jason MacLennan

"MacLennan, grab your shit and follow me!" I hear as a guard finally comes to get me out of my holding cell.

The guard is standing there looking at me expectantly, so I stand and grab my stuff, happy to finally be going somewhere beside this holding cell that I've been sitting in for the last five hours. The guard I'm following is a fat, balding guy. His neatly pressed uniform looks ironic on his sloppy body. The long, nondescript hallway we're walking down has a strange feeling to it. The walls are the color of cream and the floors are a light brown. It's almost like I've seen this hallway a hundred times before, but I've never seen this hallway before.

As we walk, the goofy guard tells me that I'm being put in segregation for a day or two because there is no space for me in the intake-unit yet. I find it incredibly unfair that I'm being put in "the hole" even though I've done nothing wrong, but by this point I'm tired and I don't care enough to protest. Plus, I've done enough time in county jail to know that any protest I make would be lost on the deaf ears of a guard who probably doesn't even see me as a human being anyway. When we finally stop, we're standing in front of a large, metal door at the end of the hallway. The guard pounds loudly on the door, and after a few seconds, another guard opens the imposing door.

As I walk through the doorway the new guard tells me to wait there for a minute. I can't help but notice that the new guard has the same sloppy look as the old one even though the new one is much thinner. I wonder to myself if being sloppy is just part of being a "corrections" officer.

The cell block is dark and loud. As I stand there, I feel like my ear drums are being beaten with a hammer from the noise. Inmates locked in their cells are yelling to their buddies who are locked in there cells all over the block. None of the individual conversations are actually discernable. They're all just lost in the mass of noise that assaults me. Little do I realize that in time this noise will start to seem normal to me.

The cell block is shaped almost like a square horse shoe. Each side has cells stretching down for an eternity, and the four tiers stacked on top of each other seem to tower above me like I'm just an ant. I can't help but think to myself how much this place looks like it belonged in a movie like "Shawshank's Redemption" as opposed to in a scene of my life. Just when I start to think that the new guard has forgotten about me, he finally comes back. He tells me to follow him as he sets off down one of the long, dark sides of the cell block.

The draft in the block gives it this strange, outside feeling to it the way a lot of buildings from the turn of the last century have. The noise is almost unbearable as we walk down the block. I've never heard anything so loud in such a small place before. The guard finally stops walking in front of a cell in the middle of the block on the bottom floor. As I peer into the cell, I'm surprised at how small and empty it is. It dawns on me that this small, concrete cage, and others just like it, is "home" now.

As I step into the cell I could see the imprints of the wooden boards in the walls and ceiling from when the concrete was poured. The old, white paint on the walls is dirty and cracked in most places. The cell is empty, except for a toilet, a sink, and a concrete bed with what looks like a workout pad on it for a mattress. There are no books and no magazines. Nothing. Just dirty concrete and steel. It seems more like the kind of place that a wild animal in a zoo might be put in rather than somewhere for a human being. Then, I think to myself that maybe that's what I am now. A wild animal locked in a cage in some type of perverse zoo. Maybe I'm not a human being anymore. I certainly don't feel like a human being anymore.

Just then my thoughts are interrupted by the roar of my cage door being slammed shut by the guard. It was the kind of loud, sickening sound of finality that only a cage door can make. The stomach-twisting sound of hopelessness. He had just shut the door on my future.

Remember You
Lavelle Mayfield

You showed me death was not a thing to fear
If I could knock down a wall, you'd still be here
I see Katz pushing on like they never knew
But I climb four tiers daily and I remember you
I put a symbol on your door, but they took it down
But I'm gone put it back again when they finish the round
If I ever find it was right to do
I'd probably make up my mind and follow you
You was a pressure player I could count on to be bolder
But this pain is sick in my body and weights on my shoulders
Or maybe it's your wings blowing down as you crossing over
When enough is enough that's what it reveals
I've got 23 letters and strawberry fields
Wish I could put the time on hold
Look at me man, just look at me
Open your eyes look around Sammie, you not alone
But you're gone
We both fought for our lives and we've had it rough
We reached for it all
But the would wouldn't give it up
I walk by the cell and look at another face
But I still see you setting there in your place
For every moment I could write pages
Now, by the 20th they say my grief will come in stages
As for that I can only guess when
So let me take a breath in
Let the pen rest for my friend
Sammie L. Johnson

Northside Minneapolis:
Avenues, Streets and Territories
Terelle Shaw

I smoked my first joint on 46th and Bryant Avenue
I smoked it with my mother and stepfather
We laughed until the early morning

I ran wild on 9th and Oliver
I stole cars and robbed homes for fun
I was bored with nothing else better to do.

I was introduced to the streets on 29th and Aldrich
I threw my bid in with committed gang members
I worked security for drug dealers and drug houses

On 24th and 4th gun battles blazed
Every one wanted control of the Four Block
I did my first bid that year

I got shot on 26th and Girard
Shortly after I got released from the Juvenile Detention Center
It was supposed to be a new me that fell victim to an old beef

I gave up on change and went back to 6th Street
It was around the way from Lowry and Lyndale
The Double L is where we sold packs 6th Street is where we laid our heads

Broadway Avenue is the heart of Minneapolis' North side
Broadway is also the gate to get to Tangle Town
That was once the headquarters before the law shut it down

31st and Newton is my last address
Now my mail reads
MCF-Stillwater, Bayport, Galley 3, cell 330, A-west

My

Ross Shepherd

I have never tasted joy,
The sweet taste of surrender filling
      My senses
Tell me that I am alone
So I can finally remove
      My mask
Hides the true me
From the judgment of
      My family
Forgives me every time
That they feel like visiting
      My grave
Is a small concrete hole
That contains nothing but
      My punishment
Ended years ago
When I finally forgot the feel of freedom and
      My joy
Is gone to a distant place
That will never be found again in
      My life
Once had meaning and purpose,
A spark of potential igniting
      My senses.

Where I am From
(inspired by George Ella Lyons)

Han Souvannarath

I am from Cluster bombs,
From Agent Orange and Napalms.
I am from the durable yellowish—brown wooden stilts
Of my grandmother's house.
I am from the opium poppies,
Bitter, yellow and sweet.

I'm from saris and sarongs,
From gold and have plenty .
I'm from the study hard and success will follow,
From respect your elders and mind your business.
I'm from giving alms every April, June, July, August
and November.
(Lighting candles and burning incense for prayers)

I'm from where elephants crowd,
Sticky rice and papaya salads.
From warring princes to the fall of a dynasty,
The life my father nearly lost protecting our ancestry.
My past, present and future a kaleidoscope of tragedies.
From the Mekong Delta, White Elephants, Lan Xang
Will forever be a distant memory.
I am from Laos.

The Mountain's Fog
Kenneth Starlin

New York will never let me go. Not that I would ever want her to but it would've been nice to have had a choice. Don't miss understand me, I loved living in New York. Not the cities or the people little of which I remember. I miss the mountains. I miss the falling snow and the solitude. I miss the quite of living isolated far away from the abrasive sounds of metal upon metal, the kinds of random banging, clanging and smashing tunes your mind is subjected to while living in the close proximity to strangers.

I long for the sense of removal I felt there in the mountains. I was only five years old and yet I remember a distinct separation that occurred between myself and the rest of the world. My new world was a world of wind dodging between fir and pine trees, playing hid and seek with me, whispering to me to explore the mountain side.

The outside world was a world of screaming angry people. A place where the ground was always pulled out from under my feet at the sound of a car door clicking shut, sealing behind it all of my mother's and my belongings safely inside for transportation to her next boyfriend's house. The door was never slammed. Slamming the door would have involved too much emotion. Instead, it was always more of an uncaring click. An ambivalent securing of a car door whose only concern is keep its occupants and their meager collection of reused boxes of belongings safe, until they reach another destination. A new house, a new home, a new place for hurting. Although my mother says there was plenty of hurting in New York.

Its odd but when I think of my life in the mountains out east I can see the rusted orange tractor above our house. I can see my BMX bike with the solid white one-piece rims. I can even see the bushy caterpillar eyebrows of my sister's grandfather as he showed me how to scoop corn kernels onto my spoon using my thumb. His eye would slightly squint as it did when he showed me something that the ladies of the house would obviously disapprove of. I even remember the corner store where my mother bought her cigarettes but I can't remember my mother's face.

At one of the happiest times in my life, why can't I grasp a single image of my mother? A single freeze frame picture of her smile or a frown or anything? My only proof I have that she was even there is the simple fact that as a five year old boy I couldn't possibly have traveled there myself.

There is another piece of evidence that New York really existed for me: His name is Chuck Martin. I know his last name because he gave my mother bruises, tears and a little baby girl: my sister, Bonnie Lynn Marie Martin. She never met Chuck. She never got to toboggan down the mountainside behind our house or wait in the snow drifts for the school bus to pick her up for the long drive to school. A trip so long we started it while the sun was still down.

I wish she could've known what it was like to float down the mountain's cool black lazy creeks. Her father and I would often canoe during the winter, after Mother Nature had forced the ice off the surface of the water. As the temperatures began to heat up, a thick fog would arise up off the lakes and creeks. A fog not like the scary ones from the movies but instead a thick wool towel that gently settles over you sheltering you from society's woes.

Sometimes, to a child's mind, I believed I was lost. Removed from every thing around me that could hurt me. Yet I had my anchor. Chuck was always there protecting me, guiding me through the clouds trapped between the mountains, chained in place to hide us from the outside world. Away from all the other men whom my mother brought around. Chuck never yelled at me, smacked me around or hurt me in the ways my mother's other crutches did.

Besides, none of them mattered any more. Chuck took us away from all of that. He took us away from the foot-hills of Colorado to the shambhala hideaway in old Tibetan legends. Where the fog guarding us grew so thick that it even held back the muffled slapping of baby waves lapping against the sides of our canoe. No small achievement when the surface of the water was only feet away from our ears.

I can still here the silence of those days. I can feel the soft muted sunshine watching over us, unseen as we floated like Aladdin down the glossy onyx river. Bonnie has never seen the skeletal silhouettes of the pine trees floating above our heads. The fog obscuring their lower trunks concealing their dirty brow needles. They floated around us like silent sentinels without a shake or rustle. Silent and ever vigilant.

How could my mother have hated all of this? How could she have taken us away from this peace? Ripped away our guardians of fir and pine. How could she have denied my unborn sister this calmness of the mountain's shadow?

She tells me a story of a time that Chuck had beaten her up so badly that I had to cook for us. She says that I had to heat canned soup for her because she couldn't eat anything else. Was I there? I don't remember this. I remember the cabin and the snowfall. The feeling of having a place. An entire mountain was our home, my place, my shelter from the hurt of the outside world. A mountain of rock and forest between us, an insulation of rivers and ice.

In the winter, creek banks would be replaced by snow. Buffers that gather along the edges of the creek, guiding her and keeping her calm along the path. The same banks that help the guardians create a silence so consuming that it seems like that entire forest is holding its breath. Waiting for the mountain to give up its secrets. To tell me if my memories are real or just my fog, protecting me from my mother's mountain.

In my memory a bridge floats into view, a low steel man-made obstacle. Cold and foreboding, coming near to soar over us. His machined ribs intruding upon our journey. Chuck had told me that this was the bridge below our house and I would only have to follow the road home if I get lost. The bridge would float around us, past us, then away. Forgotten then, but in hindsight a clear premonition of my life's larger journey. I was only five but I still feel the magic of that special place.

A was standing in a door way. I looked beyond its empty boundary and into my bedroom. Everything was stacked away in the corner leaving the painted grey floor empty, its glossy sheen mirroring the grey snow outside the window. My whole room was painted grey. Who ever thought that was a good color for a little boy's room? I only had the clothes I was wearing, not even a toy to keep me occupied during my next long journey. Everything else was packed into boxes again, but not our boxes. There would be no car door this time. All would be left behind. I took nothing with me except a child's memory because our borrowed boxes wouldn't fit on the plane back to Colorado. I would never say goodbye to Chuck, just my grey room. Outside the snow had begun to fall echoing the tones of my home. Agreeing in emotion: grey, sterile and void of warmth.

My mother had once again done what she does best. She was pregnant and we were running away. Away from the guardians that would've watched over us and kept us safe. Away from the fir and the pine that would've protected my sister when it became time for her to meet my mother's boyfriends, when she was five and I was old enough to find my own protection.

I still don't remember my mothers face, but I remember New York and the safety of the mountains that aren't mine any more.

My Mother and My Mom

Charles Yang

Though it took me months until we were properly introduced, I've known her the moment my mind took on consciousness. I enjoyed sharing each sweet, spicy, and sour taste she fed us everyday. I knew it when she was excited. I knew it when she was sad. Everyday I was forced to listen to her 80's soft rock bands and whenever I couldn't take it anymore, I gave her a good kick in the gut from the inside out. The first conversation with her consisted of a lot of screaming and crying from the both of us. We met officially on May 13th, 1984.

Strong, strict and stubborn, she is my mother. Stout, stern and short-tempered, I knew her always too quickly to bring down her hand in rage or frustration. I thought of fear from when I thought of my mother. If she were a color, it'd be red, hot and bright like coals against a hearty gust of wind. Deceptively, she stands a mere 4'9, 130 lbs. A woman of small physical stature, her authority is apparent by her commanding voice, like a page from a prison's intercom system echoing up and down the galleys.

In all my years excluding those instances where I've unexpectedly awakened her from her sleep, I've never known my mother not to have on her face and her attire properly squared. Her flamboyant taste in gaudy jewelry, artificially blackened hair — thinning and damaged from years of multiple dying and redyings and crimson lips covered always with too much lipstick betray her vanity. The tattooed-on eyebrows made it so she always looked perfectly groomed through her painted nails and toes more than often needed some touching up. Loud, arrogant and obnoxious, this is the mother my siblings and I was the most familiar with growing up.

Amongst guests and whilst entertaining company, she is comfortably charming and articulate. Often humorous, her distinct laughter is noticeably recognizable anywhere within an earshot. And matched with a smile so wide her eyes are forced closed and teeth off-white and crooked as scoliosis, she appears often quite loveable. Intelligent, clever and resourceful, she always seems to know how to remedy a problemed situation.

Abstained from smoking and drinking, a hard worker, my mother prides herself a great cook. I've never known another more prideful than her, not only of herself but of her possessions. Through her children, she kept the house clean and tidy, dishes washed and laundry always done. She allowed not one of us to leave the house to school with snot still in our eyes or our hair unkempt, our garments in disarray. In her eyes, she made no mistakes. Once, she took work off, picked me up from school and drove us 45 minutes to a dentist appointment one week early. She was furious, neither at the receptionists nor the dentist nor even at her own scheduling mishap but at me, for not having remembered the correct date of my appointment which had been previously scheduled by her six months prior. She then proceeded to give me a 45 minute lecture back to school on how hard she works and how it was my responsibility to check-up on the dates of all my appointments and if there were any discrepancies discovered that I was supposed to have let her know in advance so this sort of stuff didn't happen. I was 7 years old. I cried all the way back to school.

"I love you," was not spoken in our house. Perhaps due to my culture's conservative attitude towards affection or perhaps saying the words exposed some vulnerability in her to a degree. Brought up Catholic, she snuck in the bible and its stories to us past my father's objections that a White man should worship a White god and a Hmong, Hmong gods. I vaguely remember her tucking me in at night and coaxing me to pray to God before her style of disciplining soon drowned out the remnants of those infantile practices. Although the words were not spoken, according to her, I felt her love whenever she cracked her whip on my backside. "If I hadn't cared, I wouldn't have yelled at you or wasted the time beating you," she'd love to remind me after having just told me how much she hated me, wished I were dead, had been aborted before I were born and my skin were swollen scarlet from the welts she'd dealt me. Where the physical blows did not reach, the emotional ones were cripplingly traumatizing like a veteran scarred with PTSD. Why wasn't my mother like the ones I saw on television, like momma Brady-Bunch, Marge Simpson or that mom from The Little House on the Prarie?

In my own inherited arrogance I occasionally questioned whether she really loved me or were merely providing for me by law. It wasn't until I was an adolescent that I began to understand her style of love somewhat better. From opaque to vague, it came that I realized how tolling ten hour workdays five times a week taxed her, how costly expensive it is to clothe my five siblings and me, feed us, shelter us, medically insure us and still cook us great stomach fulfilling meals each and every night. Then, I caught this case. Sure, I'd been incarcerated before but never having faced a sentence so fatally lengthy.

My mom is loving. She is sensitive, sincere, and so soft. She cries. I've never before seen her shed tears. I actually believed she possessed no tear ducts under those bags beneath her brown eyes. So many facets to her, either she is a great liar, a con, or she's a magician and a master keeper of secrets. Funny, how after a quarter of a century you think you know someone only to be taken aback, surprised still.

It's been almost a year now since last we've seen one another in the visiting room up here at Stillwater Prison. She requests more frequent visitations except I won't allow them as long as she continues to weep for me throughout our time spent together. I call her every other weekend and find it hilarious how soft spoken she is to me one second and then tells me to hang-on another so as to set down the receiver to devour, demean and devastate those still at home with her. She'd put drill sergeants to shame.

Before this experience, when I thought of my mother, I thought of the hurt and the misery she germinated in my life. Now when I think of my mom, I see how old I've made her, of the hurt and misery I've caused to grow in her. The white hairs from stressing and the discoloration beneath the rim of her eyes obviously display countless sleepless nights on my behalf. I've so much love for this woman. I now remember that night she stayed up caring for me feeding me ice cream when I had my tonsils removed. I remember her teaching me a game with rocks and hand-eye coordination she learned when she were a little girl. I remember staying up late with mom waiting for dad to come home from work, watching late-night horror movies and cuddled up in a single blanket together both too afraid to answer the door when dad came a-knockin'.

I've come to see now the impact she's had on my life, not only in raising me but in who I've become as a person. I look in the mirror and I see so many of the same traits I listed for both resenting and respected her: strength, stubbornness, vanity, short-temperedness, intelligence, pride, honor, humor, the list goes on.

Vang Xiong Yang is my mother and my mom. I see now she is a rainbow of colors. I apologize for misunderstanding you mother, for testing you and for questioning your mothering. If not for you mom, I could never have understood myself. I thank you for your caring hands and your equally caring fists.

III.

ARTIST PORTFOLIOS

Cost of Redemption
18x24 Pastel
by C. Fausto Cabrera

Here's Your Future
18x24 Pastel
by C. Fausto Cabrera

Being Alone Series: Serene
9x12 *Pastel*
by C. Fausto Cabrera

Waiting on God
Pastel
by C. Fausto Cabrera

In the Midst of...
24x36 Acrylic
by C. Fausto Cabrera

Being Alone Series: Tranquil
Acrylic
by C. Fausto Cabrera

Young Man
Acrylic
by Kenneth Starlin

Unpacking The Box
Acrylic
by Kenneth Starlin

Afterword

Last week, a criminal court in Minnesota sentenced a seventeen year old, convicted of a gang-related killing, to life without parole after determining that life in prison for an adolescent "is neither cruel nor unusual punishment." After you read these writings, I wonder if you will agree.

Some of the writers whose work fills these pages were incarcerated as teenagers and have become men in prison. The landscape of their coming of age is shaped by craters of violence, regret, reformation, and a longing to make things right.

They tell me that it is too late for them to turn their lives around. Life without parole means no second chances. Yet, through reading and writing they have turned their minds and hearts and souls around. And, more than anything else, they want to keep other young men from the same fate.

These men reach out beyond the bars that measure lost lives. They reach out to the young men they address in the hope that their words of caution may save even one. Theirs are gestures of generosity, of selflessness, of hope. They have learned, and they have changed.

And they are writers and poets. For them, writing is the key to healing, to redemption, to the survival of the soul. In their favorite essay, "Coming into Language", Jimmy Santiago Baca writes:

> "The power to express myself was a welcome storm, rasping at tendril roots, flooding my souls cracked dirt. Writing was water that cleansed the wound and fed the parched root of my heart."

These writings, then, are the result of that cleansing: a reach outward to others in the letters to young men and a reach inward to those parched hearts in their other writing. Listen well, young women and men. They wrote for themselves and they wrote for you.

Deborah Appleman
October 15, 2009

Letters to a Young Man

... have patience with everything unresolved in your heart
and to try to love the questions themselves
as if they were locked rooms or books written
in a very foreign language.
Don't search for the answers,
which could not be given to you now,
because you would not be able to live them.
And the point is, to live everything.
Live the questions now.

~ Rainer Maria Rilke ~
(Letters to a Young Poet, translated by Stephen Mitchell)

For our next class session, Tuesday, March 17, write a letter to a young man. The young man could be anyone…your younger self, a son, or some other adolescent. (It could even be a restorative justice letter to a victim or a relative of a victim.) You can convey whatever sentiments or messages you want, but the more authentic those sentiments are, the better your piece will be.

Feel free, as we have throughout the course, to experiment with genre. In other words, your letter could be in the traditional epistolary style (that is, a plain letter!); it could be a poem; or it could be a prose piece ala wr rodriguez, Tim O'Brien, Jamaica Kincaid, or Jimmy Santiago Baca.

How long should it be? As long as it takes to say what needs to be said.

The only requirement is that the title should be "Letter to…. (you fill it in), and that the intended audience should be clear in how you title it.

Student Press Initiative Teachers College, Columbia University
Founder & Director, Erick Gordon
Box 182, 525 West 120th Street
New York, NY 10027
www.publishspi.org

Made in the USA
Charleston, SC
27 May 2010